To/Dear Janet.

Wishing you A Happy Birthday!,

Love from Lorna & Eric

July 9th — 2001.

A TREASURED MOMENT

Edited by

Rebecca Mee

First published in Great Britain in 2001 by
POETRY NOW
Remus House,
Coltsfoot Drive,
Peterborough, PE2 9JX
Telephone (01733) 898101
Fax (01733) 313524

HB ISBN 0 75432 612 8
SB ISBN 0 75432 613 6

FOREWORD

Although we are a nation of poets we are accused of not reading poetry, or buying poetry books. After many years of listening to the incessant gripes of poetry publishers, I can only assume that the books they publish, in general, are books that most people do not want to read.

Poetry should not be obscure, introverted, and as cryptic as a crossword puzzle: it is the poet's duty to reach out and embrace the world.

The world owes the poet nothing and we should not be expected to dig and delve into a rambling discourse searching for some inner meaning.

The reason we write poetry (and almost all of us do) is because we want to communicate: an ideal; an idea; or a specific feeling. Poetry is as essential in communication, as a letter; a radio; a telephone, and the main criterion for selecting the poems in this anthology is very simple: they communicate.

CONTENTS

ELEGY FOR THE COUNTRYSIDE

Come springtime when the clouds float in the sky
And we will watch the skylark sing on high.
Whilst chewing stems of grass against a wall we'll lean
Admiring far below us verdant fields of green,
And we will wonder at the nature of wild flowers
Their heads bend in the breeze as onward tick the hours,
Yet there is something missing from our tranquil view
A silence that disturbs us if we're true.
No lowing herds of cattle gently make their way
Across the fields at milking time each day.
Nor are there flocks of sheep eating their fill
Scattered across steep sides of yonder hill
And in the fields where fat pigs rooted
There is no sign of life, just stillness muted.
But this is spring the season of new birth
Yet mechanisms of death work on the earth,
As billowing smoke pours from primeval pyres
And all consuming flames dance in the burning fires,
Whilst stench of burning flesh pervades the air
Of beasts once raised by stockman's loving care.
Oh Lord make haste to bring about a peace
Who's herds contracted foot and mouth disease.
And may we learn from errors of the past
To give our green and pleasant land
A future that will last.

David A Garside

TRUE LOVE

I've never stopped
being in love.
My heart still pulsates.
I'm still alive.

If I can't love you,
then I'll love me.
And the ants
and the bees.

I'll love the ideal
of romance.
I'm in love with
the possibility of being in love.

I'm in love with
education and
generosity.
Try to understand.

I have the largest
reservoir.
A well that'll
never dry.

If I can't gush,
like a hose.
Then I'll sprinkle,
like the rain.

J Palmer

TRUE LOVE

I suppose you hurt me deeply dear,
of that I can't be sure,
no cruel words passed between us,
there was no bitter war.
Hands that held so lovingly,
did not rise and strike out blindly,
and when you broke my heart my dear,
you smiled and did it kindly.

I suppose I ought to hate, my love,
but what do I know of pain,
there are no bruises on me,
we live on both unslain.
Eyes that looked so tenderly,
looked less as we grew older,
for affections die away my love,
your gaze was dimmer, colder.

I suppose we hurt each other then,
as lovers often do,
with quiet looks and silences,
and distances that grew.
We thought we'd be together dear,
until the stars had faded,
but it is us who fade away my love,
to shadows tired and jaded.

Elizabeth Read

HIDING SORROW

I have tried not to expose raw edges,
Wounded, leaping aside, turning afraid,
I must now reduce
Bright words to bathos,
(The tender leaf perhaps quivers
In sun as well as frost),
I must quickly grasp the ordinary,
Conceal the wound sorely gaping.
You may turn your heads,
Resume our quiet conversation,
The this and that of yesterday
Dissociated from feeling,
Raw edges neatly turned under,
Hems deftly stitched.
Words must not ache
Or face distort in pain,
Tamed the revealing brush,
Dipped in thin paint,
Not throbbing out emotion
Or colour-revealed pain.

Kathleen Goodwin

FLOWERS IN A GRAVEYARD

You were my husband's mother. Yet
I have never seen your photograph
And never heard your given name.

There's no marker for your grave, so
The flowers that we bring you
May be with someone else.

Joyce Walker

REQUIESCAT IN PACE

They've laid her to rest, God rest her soul.
Queen of the ward dressed in navy blue.
The voice boomed - sergeant major at war,
God help those nurses whose nerves were raw!
Students working on her ward would quake
At every pronouncement she would make.
The techniques you either perfected
Or from her ward you'd be rejected.
Nurses mustn't show human frailties,
Counselling wasn't in her priorities!

Toilets, tables and lockers must gleam
Or woe betide the whole nursing team.
No bacterial contamination
Her ward shone with pristine perfection.
Beds were made with military precision
Envelope corners such a vision.
Drinks trolley set, precious time to save,
Medicines to give, sick people to bathe.
No stopping to chat to the patients,
That was the role of their relations!

No reprieve sneaking off to the sluice,
Sixth sense would alert her to the ruse!
Forty years have gone since we trod that ward,
The painful learning never ignored.
Lambs at the altar of vocation,
Suffer the rites of initiation.
A true professional to glory has gone.
One of a kind, her memory will live on.

Requiescat in pace, requiescat in pace.

Kathleen Potter

CRUMBS

Beside your image in me,
there is a vampire alive and kicking,
mocking whatever I think and do.
When bits of burst balloons are the outcome
of what I do, despondency attacks me,
threatening to suck any meaning.
Yet I do not give in.
You and I belong together.
Nobody, nothing can change that.
Doggedly I keep on doing my daily things,
waiting on you, my peace and love.

Angela Matheson

TARA
(1983 - 1995)

My dog, my own little friend
A mongrel it's true, but filled with love, I knew
My loneliness had come to an end.

Tiny you were, carried round in my pocket.
I loved you far more than a golden locket.
As you grew older, you sat under my arm
Looked up and kissed me, threatening all who would harm.

When out in the country, ears back, nose a-twitch,
You would smile as you jumped over grasses and ditch.
Twelve years passed by, with never a sigh,
But fate had plans for my pet.
She had a stroke, her pain made me choke
So I hastily called in the vet.

I nursed her warm body, wrapped up in a shawl
As I wrote out the cheque when the vet came to call.
'You are very brave,' the vet said, as I held her close,
My darling dog I had loved the most.

She came to me when I was in need,
Now all I have is Tara's lead.

Rosemary Whatling

OUR LOSS

How does one get over the loss of a pet,
Trying to forget her each day and yet.
Every room that you walk through you still see her there,
In the middle of the sofa or asleep on the chair.
My heart is heavy and broken in two.
Oh! My little pal, what happened to you
I loved you so much that I never thought,
Of the agony and heartbreak this day has brought.
What made you decide to cross the main road,
Were you chasing a bird or maybe a toad?
How many times I said 'Please take care,'
The thought of your loss I could never bear.
But now it has happened, and I'm filled with grief,
Your sweet little life was so very brief.
You gave endless pleasure in the short time we shared,
With your cute little antics and I know you cared.
When I sat in my chair with you on my knee
The love and affection you poured upon me.
But all this is over and your loss I mourn,
I know there are some who will probably scorn.
She's only a cat, why all the tears and fuss,
But they didn't know her, our dear little puss.
Those who have cats will know how I feel,
And it is to them that I now appeal.
Love her and cuddle her, feel her soft and warm,
And I pray tomorrow your heart isn't torn.
If you live in a village where the main road runs through,
Then all my sympathies go out to you.
Every day we have lived with this threat over our head,
One day when she is missing, we will find her dead.
It happens to others! It doesn't happen to you!
Well it does and it has, we've just lost our dear Lou.

Rita M Arksey

ELEGY OF MISTY

You had a fairly long and topsyturvy life,
When first I knew you it was mostly strife,
On market days you worked away,
No matter how you tried, you had no say.

If you did not get it right first time, then
The boot would land on your 'ahem',
You tried to please to no avail,
The passing of your owner was not a sad tale.

The landlady took over your care,
To show your appreciation, you chased all men away,
By trying to nip them on their Achilles heel,
Not always a success, it made you reel.

You had a good friend in Glen the collie,
From the same breed as you, how jolly,
You had a need to be adored,
It was a great vexation when you were ignored.

At last people got a chance to know you,
As you barked when chasing the passing cars,
This was a thing you loved to do,
Unlike getting washed, which was taboo.

Then came the brushing, this too you lapped up,
You were not averse to eating the cats' food,
Then your mistress died, when you were twelve years,
You made a new and happy home upstairs.

When walking through the cemetery,
Straight to your ex-master's grave you did go,
Where on top you would lie, as if saying,
'Who is master today?'
Misty, there is no answer to that, it is clear to see
The sadness at your passing, increases each year.

Mary Lawson

PRINCE

He was wild, he was scared.
He couldn't understand the reason
why? His Master had gone.
He looked, he searched
and could not find the one who cared,
and shared his life.

Penned up day by day whilst work was done.
Released at night sprightly and keen,
the cat he'd see, and pinned and pawed.

He settled down and came in day by day,
but still wild. He would not obey,
music settled him, he and the cat
would share a joint musical affair.

His mouth he'd gape when others came inside.
His teeth were sharp and broke the skin
of the one who would have him stay,
who tried so hard to calm him down.

But the restlessness was there,
He sought his Master still
and was wild and uncontrolled
without the voice that told him 'Stay.'

Jeni Merrifield

OUR CAT FLUFFY

A black and white ball of fluff was she
With long whiskers and pretty pink nose
Our six week old baby was called 'Fluffy'
And her beauty was just like a rose.

Her soft fur gave us both a soothing calm
And she'd never chase after the birds
She loved to curl up in the warmth of our arms
And hide where she couldn't be heard.

Our Fluffy would lie on her back for a rub
And her tummy felt soft and smooth
But to see any water or go near a tub
She'd escape like a kangaroo.

She dipped her paw in a tin to eat
And pinched straws out of Mummy's cup
Fluffy walked off with pens gripped in her teeth
Played our piano to make us wake up.

She killed our fish and bit their tails off
Then hid them inside Laura's shoes
But how could we get angry and look very cross
When we saw Fluffy's innocent-look blues?

Our love grew so strong over 14 years
Fluffy seemed to sense my distress
She'd sit by my face and lick up the tears
And look right into my eyes from my chest.

At her funeral 18 people were here
Many people had suffered her loss
The piano was played as we sang through the tears
She'd been poisoned and died at a cost.

Nearly three years have passed since our Fluffy died
But we know we'll forget her - never
She gave so much love; enriched all our lives
Now in Heaven she'll live forever.

Virginia M Z Haymond

MY DARLING SOOTY

I knew you were deteriorating when you didn't eat or drink
Not touching your favourite chicken -my hopes began to sink.
Didn't think you'd make it through the long, dark night ahead,
So I crept down in the early hours, hoping you were not dead?
You were, as usual, on your stool - you seemed glad to see me too
I couldn't let you die alone and I didn't know what to do.
So worried about you was I - I took you to work next day
We spent our time together - you heard me as I prayed.
You nosed around my office and had a look outside
Then gladly went back to your box and I could just have died.
To know you were no better - not a bit like my old Soot
Your lovely face, your amber eyes, the adoring way you looked.
I later took you to the vet, he couldn't help at all
Except to treat you kindly - my heart began to fall.
I was with you when you slept at last, my tears just blinded me
We cut some of your fur off, for me to cherish tenderly.
Next day was such a bad one - my Precious Bundle on my lap
As I took you to the Sanctuary, my dear beloved, treasured cat.
I wrote into the little book, not knowing what I penned
My poor old heart just broken - my Sooty at his end.
I kissed your little face again and placed you in the box
How could I bear to part with you - I plundered to the rocks,
And there I had to leave you, but you'll be back with me I know -
I'll cherish your ashes deeply, you'll be with me when I go.
Without you in the home at all, I'm all at sea and lost
My life so devastated - just thrown about and tossed -
On the broad horizon, I miss you each and every minute
My life so wrecked and torn about - without my Sooty in it.

Iris Cone

ELEGY TO AN URBAN FOX

Sneaky, slinking, furtive thing
Quick to pounce then slide away
Grey wraith slipping, moonlight lit
Both hearts pound in this foray.

Den and cubs call, you turn and circle
Warily, with muzzle full.
White flash of throat a shock in darkness
My reward for night's vigil.

But daylight brings another traffic -
Unending hum, uncaring road.
Truckers pound with dusty menace,
Flashing metal, murderous load.

Stay clear - life is unequal here -
Headlights see not, soft fur, warm breath.
Unstreetwise as you are vulpine
Out here the referee is death.

Were you my sneaky, slinking, wraith-like friend?
Dimming glory of a red-gold coat
Black-tipped tail, sharp ears limp
Muzzle snarled above white flash of throat?

I hope to see you, I need to love you.
For both of us the end is death.

Lilian Perriman

IN MEMORY OF WORKING DAYS
(After Hillaire Belloc)

Do you remember the lab
Diego
Do you remember the lab?
And the joking and the crying
The teasing and the smirking
When we should have been working
And the gossiping all through the day?
And the moans and the groans when things went astray
(And why was it always you to blame?)
Do you remember the lab Diego,
Do you remember the lab?
And the moans and the groans when things went wrong
Causing lots of hassle,
Don't hang about to listen
To the bore who thought he knew it all!
And the Slip! Slap! Slop!
Of the ice
On your neck, melting, cold and wet
And the girls gone sharking,
Flirting,
Shagging.
Groping and hoping,
Dancing at a party in a spin
Drunk as skunks!
You had to be mad to work there!
Do you remember the lab
Diego
Do you remember the lab!

Never more,
Diego
Never more.
You have left us all:
And only memories remain.
In the long winter days
I'll recall your Spanglish ways
And think that for someone else you're a pain!
Evermore!
Evermore!

L A Churchill

AN ELEGY: FOR OSCAR WILDE

You gave them beauty,
Shimmering in your verse,
In strangely-wrought, fantastic fairytales,
In lyrical prose-poems.
All your words
Wove magic in the fabric of grey lives -
So the mundane and monochrome
Flamed out jewelled loveliness.
Your voice, they said, was golden,
Gentle, sweet,
Like water bubbling in a silver jar,
Whispering of ancient mysteries,
Scarlet and purple dreams.
Ah! how we too need your enchanted dreams,
We whose poor, narrow lives are vainly passed
In empty busy-ness and care-dulled days.
You give us beauty.

Jackie Lapidge

EPITAPH

Consider her greatness
Denied the leverage to lead;
Although her soul
Throbbed like a cello
In every breath
Of super-sensory thought
And goaded her fragility.

Consider how she knew
The vagrancy of infant minds
And when those shadows,
Blacker than deodars
Against the garish backdrop
Of a swooping Eastern sun
Peopled the nursery night;
With naked candle and naked words
She swept them up into the cracks
That pattered across the ceiling,
Where shuddering,
They cowered until you slept,
Then danced again within your brain.

Consider how she walked,
Offering to all she knew
Exquisite blooms,
Whose petals fall
Softer than snowflakes
On the crystalline floor of dreams.

Consider her greatness
Which lives on in the mind
Though flesh is banquet
For the worms and time.

Jeffrey A Pickford

GOD'S CHILD

Thou wert given to me for seven years,
to help me endure heartaches and tears.
God knew that I had need of thee,
He sent you in mercy and compassion to me.
Our Lord God's number is but seven,
God's number of completeness given from heaven.
Seven precious years my Lord did lend,
When his canine child to me did send.
Happy were they glorious days,
filled with love and sunshine's rays.
Thy faithful friend so loyal and true,
gave his undying love and joy anew.
One night our Lord saith 'My dear,
I needeth my little one back, I fear.'
Just before our Lord Jesus' birth,
God took my little dog from the earth.
The gift He'd asked for during my prayer,
Barney thy precious one back in thy care.
Although mine heart breaketh in two,
I picture my precious one joyful with you.
Lord I thanketh Ye for years numbering seven,
that you lendeth thy little one from heaven.
Surely Lord soon, a new heaven and earth,
a time for repentance and new rebirth.
What joy to encounter thy glorious face,
and my loved one in Thy heavenly place.

N Young

POMPEII

Marble white pillars stand bathed in the sun,
Back into time where a memory begun,
Once was a city of splendour and might,
Pompeii, the name of the constant delight.

Romans' built villas, with gardens and fountains,
Beautiful frescoes, adorning surroundings,
Life blossomed on through each colourful season,
Came an eruption for some unknown reason.

Buried, this jewel, inside Mother earth,
Keeping so safe, to preserve all her worth,
Then Nature came back with another brave hand,
Found countless treasure; by uncovering this land.

Saved in a capsule of time; so that we,
Return to an age yet unequalled to see,
The glory of Rome, as it was long ago,
City of Pompeii, how I loved you so.

Pauline Evans

ELEGY

*(A Tribute to Derek Blundell
Elder of Bethel Baptist Church,
Whitchurch, Cardiff)*

Each generation puts faith to the test
Searching and seeking, they never can rest
But doubt clouds belief, so someone must lead
To rebuild the hope of a people in need.
In a world full of hate, morals are lost
Servants are needed who count not the cost
What kind of person could stand up this way
Facing the pain of derision each day?

Derek, our Elder, so full of God's grace
The deep love of God shone forth from his face
So proud that his faith was shared by his wife
Gold veins of compassion ran through his life.
Derek, our brother, so strong and sincere
Surely God chose him and guided him here
Through all the pain he stood firm in Your way
That is why Bethel is still here today.

Thank you Lord Jesus
For a friend who was true
So sure of his faith,
And now resting with You.

Henry Dunn Williams

ELEGY TO MY LORD

How must it have felt that awful day?
When power of people held dread sway,
By demanding to be given
He who was their path to Heaven.
Seeing crowd so much increase,
Pontous Pilate did release,
Saying this man's soul is white,
No sin at all on it lays blight.
People pushed crown on Lord's head,
Causing rents which fiercely bled.
Made a cross, found long sharp nails,
Forced him to carry, which entailed.
Struggling walk up green hillside,
Where Peter thrice his Lord denied.
Three men nailed to crosses there,
Then cross put upright in the air,
Thieves on other crosses cried
'He is God's Son for brave He bides.'
Our sins were why He suffered there,
How felt they causing such despair?
By nailing Him to cross that day
On a green hill far away.
How would those people sleep each night?
Remembering that awful sight.
Three men arms held fast by nails
Another which their feet impales.
When up Ghost God's dear Son gave,
They could not keep Him in the grave.
He rose and now two centuries on,
We love and worship still God's Son.

Barbara Goode

BALLIOL REMEMBERED

To wake from just and worldly sleep
And, memories of pleasure-filled dreams abound
Anticipating the ecstasy of a future passed
On this heaven-sent, clay-clad mound.

To walk betwixt His wondrous gifts
Revelling in long-lost freedom found
Then, dashing there and dancing here
As the day unfurls, and breath allows.

To speak with friends most cherished
And, talk of ancient times to come
Of deeds well done and comfort shared
Lives lived amid that glorious enchantment.

To drink a cup, fresh brewed
Or, a glass of spirit, Scottish through
And, feel the living flesh refreshed
The flagging vessel once more renewed.

To think slight thoughts in perfect truth
Knowing those who played each vital part
And, remembering every separate, joyful act
As if those moments were never wholly spent.

Yet, Balliol is still gone; but not forgotten
His every wish lives deep within our heavy hearts
We will remember him; our lives He surely touched
And, meet once more upon the dew-drenched glen.

Stan McKerron

THE ELEGY

God bless Don Quixote and Sancho Panza
For being adventurous
So long ago

God bless his horse Rosinante
And Sancho Panzas
They had to go

Like animals of the world
They do their share
You cannot ask for more

As the cows that Dad and his friends
'Milked' if they could
In the front line - in the First World War

Phyllis O'Connell Hampson

FERRYMAN'S COTTAGE

Alas! It is no more - it is sadness, indeed
Cottage and garden derelict to nature's weed,
but there is still sweet peas and a rose in flower
could but these walls tell of their finest hour,
when folk would need to cross the Severn water
ferryman rows, and the boy guides with rudder.

Gone are those days of yore
when ferryman and boy rowed from shore to shore,
those days in mind I see
when river life was hard but time was free,
of sad times and those that were merry
whilst waiting your turn for the ferry,
the children played in fields and ran
the river folk passed news to the ferryman.

To feel sorrow about those days bygone
is to know that in memory we are not alone,
for time, is but a space in which we dwell
as this derelict cottage here could tell,
as homeward, I have my steps to turn
from this a forgotten life, to be left forlorn.

John Clarke

SAD FAREWELL

To tonsils, removed when I was eight
Large, sore constantly, good riddance

To appendix, tricky little organ
Taken when I was thirty-ish

To my ageing uterus, bye bye!
Temporary bereavement

To teeth, one by one, pulled
I *did* clean, floss, visit the dentist

To 20:20 vision, faded when?
Now, I wear glasses, that's okay.

To blonde hair, stopped plucking grey
Just dye it, don't want to be bald!

To supple joints and muscles
Try to creak and grind in rhythm

To smooth peachy skin
Wrinkles increase when I grin

Minus so many bits and pieces
It hasn't stopped me forging ahead

Life is such a precious gift
No matter what, I try to enjoy it

Peggy Billett

ELEGY FOR A LIFER

I interviewed him for release -
I'd never seen him smile:
He'd been unknown to Police -
That never was his style.

So long ago he'd judged his wife
Of faithlessness (in error!).
Despite her pleas he took her life,
Impervious to her terror

Two sons he smothered as they slept,
A daughter was the other
Whose life was saved by being kept
That night with her grandmother.

His unsuccessful suicide,
Like mark God left on Cain,
Bequeathed a brand he could not hide;
He walked henceforth as lame.

He sought no camaraderie,
Unpardoning, unpardoned.
Amid the lifer's coterie
He walked apart and hardened.

I never have before or since
Encountered such despair -
A man who would quite clearly wince
If I ever showed some care.

Although I failed to reach him,
I concluded by and large
He had died as had each victim.
I recommended his discharge.

He came to me, his arms outflung,
'You tried to be my minder.
For what I did I should have hung!
To me you'd have been kinder!'

He soon achieved his expiation:
Smashed body on the rocks
Perhaps allayed his soul's striation
And broke his chains and locks.

The Governor, a clergyman and I,
Supporting one another
Were joined at the cremation by . . .
A lady and grandmother.

I rue my efforts, ineffectual
To give him hope, rebirth . . .
I failed this man, dysfunctional,
Who'd been serving Hell on Earth!

Patrick Brady

A LINCOLNSHIRE ELEGY

From Horncastle, William Marwood came
He had a cobbler's shop,
Mark well this, his claim to fame
He invented the Marwood knot!

In the year of eighteen-eighty,
To William Gladstone (who was PM)
The Secretary for Ireland said -
'Sir, I feel I ought to go
This Kitty O'Shea, Parnell affair
It's unsavoury, you know.'

Sir Frederick Cavendish
He filled the vacant post,
With colleague T H Burke he sailed
West, to Ireland's coast.

Next day, in Dublin's Phoenix Park,
There they strolled, had a talk.
For them it was the final walk
Their violent end brought consternation
To current 'Home Rule' negotiations
(It's 2001 and still no reconciliation!).

Four men, guilty they were found
Of the crime in Phoenix Park,
Against Sir Frederick Cavendish
And companion T H Burke.

You ask 'What links these sad events
With Marwood's cobbler's shop?'
Is just as well you do not know,
It is the 'Hangman's Knot'!

Bill was England's public hangman
For him the die was cast.
The four he hung in Dublin's jail
They were to be his last.

There in Lincoln's waiting room,
His Horncastle train to catch,
Bill Marwood collapsed and died,
His gruesome life was passed.

Amid the panic-stricken babel,
Occupying a nearby table
Mollified by what they say,
Incognito, there they sat
Irish Patriots (they'd tracked him back).
Bill Marwood's avowed assassins
Thoughts and deeds fired by hate
Their vengeful act now denied them
By a macabre stroke of fate.

G Nicklin

YELLOW FISH

(This verse is dedicated to my granddaughter Rebecca,
who died June 2000, age 10 years, after bravely fighting
a difficult illness. Yellow Fish is the name she gave herself,
as she felt it described the way she looked after her treatment)

They came and took my little Yellow Fish away,
Where she's gone I cannot say.
Up in Heaven we hope and pray,
With all the other children that went that day.

I cannot sing her favourite song
Or laugh and joke all day long.
Winter's here and here to stay,
Birthdays, Christmas, every day.

Pay-days come and pay-days go,
I cannot pay my little Yellow Fish,
Though she has earned the greatest wage of all,
For her love and lessons to us all.

So up in Heaven Rebecca sits,
With her treasured box of little bits,
Little bits of this and bits of that,
In her box I could not see, all the love she gave to me.

I only hope, one day to see
Her smiling face looking back at me.
For all the precious things we bear,
Mean nothing when you are not there

Now my little Yellow Fish can only be,
The brightest star that I can see.
Her courage and love for one so young,
Was greater than the morning sun.

Her last words were to her mum,
'Loving You', and then was done.
Her love, our love will never die,
We'll meet upon the morning sky.

All my Yellow Fish's love
Was far too great to make me bitter and hate.
So great spirit help me see, why Yellow Fish no more can be?
So great spirit help me see, why these things have to be?

W J Oliver

ELEGY TO MY ADOPTIVE PARENTS

Sweetly on the air it drifts,
That song from childhood's age,
Bringing back times of long ago
When love turned every page.
Someone, somewhere, cannot know
How that sound makes my senses ache,
Playing the song you used to sing
Till I feel my heart will break.
Love there's been since you both died
That is very dear to me,
But none can fill the cold dark void
That was left when you ceased to be.
Like rocks you were, steadfast and true,
My harbour in life's storm.
Safe in your love, no matter what;
Your gift a priceless one.
All this I know, and thank you
From my loving grateful soul.
My tragedy?
Not understanding this
Till both of you were gone.

Joy Sanders

ALWAYS IN MY THOUGHTS

No words can I find to ever express or to say
How much my darling I miss you in every way
You are always in my thoughts remembered each day
I carry the sweet memories of you along my life's pathway
In that special place deep, deep inside my heart
Where your memory will always be so, we'll never be apart
Sometimes I see your kind and loving face
When I close my eyes to sleep next to your empty space
That's when I know that you are near
Comforting me with your love, telling me you're still here.

Elizabeth Leach

REMEMBER

We weep for all the men who gave their lives,
Remember families deprived
Of seeing sons or brothers mature
Because their deaths were premature,
Fathers who did not see first or last child,
Nor the sparkling eyes when baby smiled
They sleep under white crosses in war graves,
Have we proved worthy of peace they gave?

From all continents came keen volunteers,
Those conscripted left in good cheer,
Beforehand some had not strayed village,
Soon embarked troopship, hush-hush voyage,
All battlegrounds fought by three armed forces,
To keep world free with merged resources,
They sleep under white crosses in war graves,
Have we proved worthy of peace they gave?

Do you think of life for them at eighteen?
To see death, injuries obscene,
No life! Camaraderie sustained,
Eased horror and getting crackbrained.
Red poppies are men, some suffered torture,
Youngsters became men without future,
They sleep under white crosses in war graves,
Have we proved worthy of peace they gave?

Mothers and wives received telegrams
The dreaded paper said 'We regret Ma'm . . . '
Millions of planted white crosses
World over, each died a violent death for us.

Hilary Jill Robson

AN UNCLE OF WHOM I NEVER KNEW

Your light has gone, and with it much you knew.
The sadness that engulfed your life has left a residue.
And now those who were unknown to you, belated mourn,
For we did not even know that you were born.
We did not know of your existence until recently,
But sadness for our loss will no less be.
Sadness for you, because rejection was to be your fate.
As now we learn of your existence, for you too late.
You were my uncle, rejected as a child.
No fault of the 'just born', but fate decreed, society reviled.
Your mother gave you up, we know she was so young.
No blame to her, I'm sure she loved her newborn son.
And now I'm learning from your nearest family,
Of the effect of this rejection, and how you came to be
Saddened and withdrawn from them, those who cared;
And now realising the reason, they are aware.
For they had begun to research their family tree,
And in this way revealed your past, your history.
Now we, as a family, two sides of the same coin -
Can come together, to understand and mourn.

Jean Rosemary Regan

In Memory Of Abbie-Jade

My heart is sad, my heart is numb
Now our Abbie-Jade has gone
We gave her love, much more than enough
But she couldn't stay to receive that love.

She gave us hope, she gave us joy
We wouldn't have minded if she were a boy
Memories of that wee small babe
She was our little Abbie-Jade.

To have stayed, we dearly wish she could
To experience life with her mum and dad
We'd have cherished her all day long
But can only remember, now she has gone.

A much loved child she would have been
A special grandchild and niece
We said goodbye and laid her to rest
Our dear Abbie-Jade, you were the best.

God will tend to you every day
And comfort you in every way
He's held you special in his heart
Since that day you did depart.

Mummy and daddy must get some rest
And promise that we'll do our best
To come to terms with the fact that you're gone
And spend some special time to mourn.

Your little body, so perfect
Is one that we will never forget
God love our daughter as we do
What she is to us, let her be to you.

Goodnight, God bless, our little babe
We hope to meet with you someday.

Kate Sorby

SHEPHERD BEN MURRAY

I imagine that you would have been
A quiet country boy then,
Only in photographs I have seen,
The shepherd *Murray Ben.*

The SanQuar hills of mist and fog,
In a morning peaceful glen,
A working, panting collie dog,
By the side of shepherd *Ben.*

I can almost see your smiling face,
As I walk through the Scottish thistle,
Feel the warmth of your embrace,
And the sound of your shepherd's whistle.

You would have been a great wee fiddler,
'Danny Boy' you always sung then,
To your best friend 'Wee Tiddler'
The love of shepherd *Ben.*

So dark and handsome with dog and crook,
An honest, canny type,
Your life, an unfinished storybook,
As your wee broon smokin' pipe.

As the heather blaws in the country air,
And the grass sits with morning dew,
Your presence is felt almost everywhere,
As I fondly think of you.

I can almost hear the fiddle play,
By the fire in your *'But an Ben'*
I just wish that I could find a way
To bring you back *Dear Ben. xxx*

Rosemary Gladwell

THE LAST BATTLE

No more I glance his solid frame,
His presence is removed.
No more his laughter, echoing,
This soldier, I did love.

His soul is drifting far away,
Approaching Heaven's door.
His weary time of combat,
Has passed for evermore.

This clever man of diverse charms,
Now rides the ferryboat.
Into the land of dreaming,
Across God's timeless moat.

Now his arduous days are done,
His wandering soul will rest.
And though I miss him dreadfully,
His memories are the best.

Duchess Newman

AFTER MEGAN

What words are there that I can use
Now that you've gone from me?
I do suspect that there are none
To ease the misery
Which permeates my heart and soul
And clouds my grieving mind
'Til I'm uncertain of my role
In the life you've left behind.

For you are dead whilst I remain
Distressed and lost and low,
Receiver of impatient looks
From those who do not know
The life we shared, the love we had,
The bond that held us tight;
Now memories are all I have
To take into the night

Of life.

Brian Beveridge

TO MUM

I thought of you yesterday,
As I watched the birds searching for food.
Tiny, defenceless, relying on others
In times of need -knowing that help will be there
As I was for you.
Just knowing, makes them free.
Giving them hope for tomorrow,
And when tomorrow comes -
To be held, gently, until it is time
To take flight and be lifted up to freedom
Where troubles fall away, like ribbons around a gift.

Our gift is love.
A constant love, infinite and forever.
Simply biding time now
Until once again, mother and child are reunited.
In a dewy pasture of another world.
Safe in the bright shining light, which is love.
Yes, I thought of you yesterday
And I thought of you today
I miss you.

Sharon Stead

FIRST LOVE

First kiss was sweet as honey
First touch like summer rain
First night we had no money
First love please come again
First passions for each other
First glimpse of what love meant
First warning from my mother
First feelings Heaven sent
First words to say I love you
First day we had a fight
First loneliness without you
First long and sleepless night
First told you loved another
First time you had to go
First one to be my lover
First love I miss you so.

Elizabeth Hopkinson

HAPPY TIMES - QUESTION MARK

From the day that I was born,
no one did I scorn.
Folk would travel miles
just to glimpse at one of my smiles!
I was always rather a happy
little chappy.
Of all the things that I possess,
the most cherished one is happiness.
All the good times we had,
just me and my dad!
It was always December
that I seem to remember,
when the snow lay everywhere deep.
Through the night we would sleep
after playing with my cars,
or merely gazing up at the stars!
Then by day,
we would play
- football on the lawn
or go fishing at dawn!
From Mum we would hide
and on his back I would ride,
when I was a cowboy!
'Aye, aye, cap'n - ship ahoy!'
When out at sea
we'd pretend to be!
Sometimes we'd sit for a while
and simply just smile
at each other
and have a laugh with my mother!
However, Dad was killed when I was two!
So all these things we never had chance to do
and now the memories grow dim,
but I really do love him!

Michael W Williams

ELEGY TO BOB SHAW

I think of you - and firstly I see,
Crinkly blue eyes, smiling down on me,
Naughty boy, with mischievous whit,
Never to hurt, - just stirring a bit!
It's hard to accept, you're no longer here,
You're sadly missed, though I know you're near!

You did your best to be a good provider,
For Edna and children - a rock beside her.
He never quite made it as Bob the Builder!
Hinges and cupboards together bewilder . . .
Even though, you've left us, for a short while,
We'll all get together and those eyes'll smile.

The Shaws of Sale are dwindling down,
Your family still renowned in town.
We only knew - you were born by the Vine,
Now raise your Guinness to the great Divine!
Our lives have been touched by your gentle laughter,
You'll brighten upstairs - in Heaven hereafter.

Patricia Derbyshire

Feel, Encore, Out
(Do I Feel Abandoned or Released?)

My closest friend;
my living nightmare.
I'll love you and break you,
miss you and hate you.

You've lived with me for years,
taught me everything and how to cope;
helped me through my fears.
And now I'm losing you forever.

A while ago I wanted to be dead.
You made me think that was right,
but then, you controlled my head.
Now they're sending you away.

Once, we coexisted in harmonious relief:
I relied on you for everything,
but now you're destroying me from the inside:
the place I thought I was strongest.
I'm sorry but you have to go:
the tablets are slowly killing you.

The further down you pushed me,
the more I needed you.
You never let me reach the bottom,
So my terror never left.

We went through so much together,
I think of you every day.
It feels strange living without you,
my closest friend.

Anna Robertson

MY DAD

How dare you dad, you have no right.
To leave me here to cope and fight.
I'm all alone I need you so.
My dearest dad why did you go?
This awful pain that's in my heart.
It will not go, now we're apart.
I'm sorry Dad my selfish view,
I thought of me and not of you.
It hurt me dad to see your pain,
One day I know we'll meet again.
You gave us all your dearest love.
And if you could, the moon above.
I thank you Dad the start in life,
You gave to us will ease our strife.
You're safe and well your pain has gone.
This lovely thought will keep me strong.
I miss you dad I love you so.
While we're apart my love will grow.
It does not end in me I know
Memories of you will never go.

Christine Ianson

GLEAM IN HIS EYE

Surely conceived in a thunderstorm,
He moved too fast from the day he was born.
Benzedrine quick-silver flowed in his veins,
It powered his limbs, kindled his brain
To the loudest laughter, from the deepest pain:
Dodging headlights on a short-cut across the sky,
With an angel's blindspot gleam in his eye.

He carved a career out of pushing his luck,
Like double or nothing he had to come unstuck.
Harebrained schemes launched by twisting an arm,
Whole shaky enterprises held up with charm -
How long could it go on before he came to some harm?
Heard the sound of the hounds as the fox raced by,
With an angel's blindspot gleam in his eye.

With some crazy notion of beating the odds,
He dumped the whole bundle in the lap of the Gods;
Nicotined fingers crossed - minimal nails -
A million pound cargo if the boat could only sail.
Heading for a long holiday if this one fails:
We watched and we wondered how nothing could belie
That same old angel's blindspot gleam in his eye.

Then suddenly the sand-glass had finished its flow,
And Mother Earth came to collect on the loan.
They gathered in salute from all over his world,
Out of the pack fell three boys and a girl;
As the clinging mist became a cascade of pearls
The line of his legacy said their goodbyes,
With an angel's blindspot gleam in their eyes.

Mark Tuck

A SUNBEAM FOR JESUS

Andrea, you had special charms
laughing, crying or waving your arms.
A *Sunbeam* sent to your brother and me
we did not know how special you'd be!
Soon learning to drink from a cup
determined you were to sit up,
Mum was bathing you one day,
she pointed out a scar on your spine,
which looked just like a thin line.
You were bright and could talk,
Mum said you might not ever walk.

Then back from hospital came some news,
an iron brace, and special shoes,
could possibly aid you to walk.
You would try, there was a chance,
to learn to walk, or even dance!
The last words you said to me
were 'Don't go out tonight She!'
Mum said 'You must let Sheila go,
she's played all day with you I know.'

When I got home there was a note,
and a lump came to my throat.
You had not been well at all,
that night to Heaven you took your charms
and fell asleep in Mum's arms.
Your headstone's a Bible inscribed with the words
A Sunbeam for Jesus, This came true
when at eight and a half to Heaven you flew.
Where a *Sunbeam* lives life anew.

Sheila Walters

MOTHER

Who was there to dry our tears,
Who was there to calm our fears
Who was there to help us walk
Who was there to teach us to talk?
Mother

Who held our hand on our way to school
Who taught us how to keep our cool
Who bandaged knees, wiped bloody nose
Who cuddled us and held us close?
Mother

Who spent nights by our sick bed
Holding our hand, cooling our head.
Reading a story till we fell asleep
Waiting till dawn, then out she'd creep?
Mother

Thank you Mum for your loving care
Thank you for the joys we shared.
Thank you just for being there.
Wishing that you were still here.
Mother

Muriel Johnson

GOODBYE KEN

Together we stood on the day that
we did marry.
By my side you stood as your children
I did carry.
Together there we stood
as our child was laid to rest,
And never have I loved anyone in the
way that I loved you.
Yet never have I hated anyone in the
way that I hated you too.
I could not live with you, yet I could
not live without you.
Now to see you laid to rest is the
hardest thing I'll ever have to do.

M A Shipp Yule

MY MUM'S OLD ROCKING CHAIR

I look at Mum's old rocking chair
And often wished that she was there,
It seems unfair now she has gone.
That it's so hard to carry on
Amid the chores of every day.
Oh Mum, dear Mum, what's left to say?
I miss you nights, I miss you days,
I miss you in so many ways.

I look at that old rocking chair,
So still it looks in deep despair.
As if to say come on sit down,
You're tired with shopping, burdened down.
Rest your head start counting sheep,
And I will rock you off to sleep.
And Molly will sing you a lullaby,
Hush pretty moma now don't you cry.

Let me kiss your wrinkled brow,
Oh Mum, dear Mum, where are you now?
I often cry myself to sleep,
Though missing you, I'll always keep
Your sweet dear photo in my heart.
Close to me to never part.
I'll sit in your old rocking chair,
And pretend my love, you're always there.

Ian Proctor

ELEGY - TO MY LOVED ONE

Alas my love the time is here
  When all I have are memories dear.
The presents bought through many years
  Do help, although they bring the tears.
But nevertheless my thanks I give
  For many blessings given when you did live
And cherish me with all your love
  Before you went to heaven above.
Your photographs still give to me
  A mountain of memorability.
As now I look to days of yore,
  You're in my heart for evermore.
Once again my thanks to you I send
  With the certain knowledge that in the end,
You'll be there to greet me on the shore
  Of God's heavenly kingdom - together once more.

Jean C Pease

IF I COULD HAVE KNOWN

I say 'Goodbye'
I will see you again.

I take you for granted
Always knowing I will see you again.

I believe you'll be there for me
Soon, I will see you again.

Then the day comes.
I couldn't have imagined it would be the last time.

I didn't say it with enough feeling
'Goodbye'
I will never see you again.

Helen Riley

To Mother

(To my dear Mother
31st May 1904 to 2nd January 1998)

Oh sad is my heart this wretched day,
As I follow her coffin on its woeful way.
My mother now lies there at peace within,
She died so old, so feeble and so thin.

She lived a full life until the age of ninety-three,
Using each moment of her life enthusiastically.
Though her eyes had dimmed, her mind was sharp,
Her body had aged, but she was young at heart.

When I looked upon her inert and shrunken form,
I look back to the day when she had been born.
She was once a child so bright, happy and gay,
Whose flaxen hair tossed as she ran to play.

She blossomed into a beautiful blushing girl,
Dashing through life, causing hearts to whirl.
At last finding true love with her handsome beau,
She walked down the aisle with a radiant glow.

She raised two daughters and also a son,
Who knew they'd a caring and loving mum.
When times were hard, she kept her head,
She worked and slaved to see her children fed.

A compassionate mother, and a loving wife,
Preparing us all for the trials of our future life.
Her boundless energies conquered every call,
In kitchen, garden, music, art, she'd done them all.

So when next you see someone slow with aged frame,
Do not treat them with impatience or disdain.
They've accomplished more than you'll ever know,
And earned the right to be worn out and terribly slow.

John Mitchell

ELEGY ON FRIENDSHIP

No words can say how much I miss you
My dear, dear friend, but memories,
Of all we meant to each other
Will never fade.
We met when you were gently ageing,
Your soldier's past was plain to see
In your code of honour and integrity.
Your kindness and humour undimmed
Your smile was like the sun,
In its sweet radiance
You eyes so very blue.
By your very presence,
You helped me when anxious and alone,
To face a happier future.
Dear friend, my son and I both loved you
For your guidance and concern,
We miss you every day
But you have left a warmth,
Within my heart to stay.
As love and friendship cannot die
We shall meet in Heaven I trust,
No longer will I miss you
But rejoice in new life,
A loving friendship renewed.

Elisabeth Morley

SPECIAL LOVE

I miss you my darling
I'm grateful for the life
You shared with me
Your kind and caring ways
I sometimes failed to see
Our love was special
We had times of passion and pain
Farewell my love
Until we meet again . . .

Christa Todd

BEHIND CLOSED DOORS

We will never know the long, dark road
That led, it seems, nowhere.
Your worries and troubles a tiresome load
Too much for you to bear.

Your laughter brought joy to all you knew,
Your smile - so bright and gay.
Your kind, caring ways gave folk hope anew
To face another day.

Not once did you fail to find the time
To help some other soul:
Lending a shoulder, an ear, sometimes
Such favours took their toll.

You could not believe the love and respect
Our village for you held.
Those down-trodden years had taken effect,
Your love for life had quelled.

Outside, and to others, you put on 'the face'
That one and all adored.
Inside you felt sorrow and hurt and disgrace,
And cried, behind closed doors.

Helen Gavin

END OF THE WORLD

Sleep my baby sleep
While the storm rages around us
Dream my baby dream
While the world comes to an end
Die my baby die
Find my arms your peaceful cradle
Fly my baby fly
Like my perfect little angel
Rest my baby rest
In the lap of Jesus Christ
Live my baby live
In the safety of God's eye
Wait my baby wait
Till I find you once again
And love my baby love
As you soothe a mother's pain.

Linda Catherine Hind

My Son

My children are my joy I have a
Little son with rosy cheeks
And a sturdy little boy.
The only sadness that I have
Is they will never know a Dad.
But even with his handicap
I will see they don't turn bad.
I will work my fingers to the bone
To give them what they need,
And hope that when they
Reach adult age they both will
Prosper and succeed.

Roger Brooks

IN MEMORY

(Dedicated to the Air Show pilot.
So many I have known and lost)

Soar high on silver wings,
Reach above the clouds
And never look down.

And listen . . .
As the piston engines roar.
Crash dive, pull back!
No use, you died.

And for what? Who?
We, the public,
Who came to see your show,
Or because it was your life?

We watch and we feel,
And we think we feel,
The nostalgia of the era.

In death's dark vale
Can you see the light?
Your machine is waiting.

Fly high on silver wings,
Soar high onto Heaven,
As we remember you.

Angela G Pearson

MY LOVE FOR YOU

I loved you, how I loved you
      With love so pure and true.
Although you have gone before me,
      I am still in love with you.

We were not in love, when first we met,
      Our love had to grow.
Each time we met, the spark was there,
      The seed of love, we had to sow.

We were engaged on that January day
      When I was just twenty-one.
We married two years later
      Then true love had begun.

You worked very hard, at your job
      To keep us both, as you could.
You didn't grumble at long hours,
      But I knew you never would.

We kept our love on an even keel
      When trouble came our way,
You were always sympathetic
      And taught me to live, and love, always.

I looked up to you, and honoured you,
      You were solid as a rock.
You could always find an answer,
      When others would only mock.

When illness came to weaken you
      Your spirit never crumbled.
You suffered much, towards the end,
      I never heard you grumble.

We never made our Golden Day,
      Each day was golden to me.
We'll meet again, I know we will.
      When our love will shine, for all to see.

Joan Smith

MUM - ALWAYS IN MY HEART

Mum, you left so suddenly
We couldn't say 'Goodbye'
I don't know how I'll manage
As the years go slowly by.

We were so very much alike,
We couldn't show our love.
I only hope that now you're gone
You're watching from above.

Many a time I lie awake
And wonder if you knew
How very much I loved you;
How much I needed you.

You gave love to my children
And warmed them with your praise.
Gave comfort when I needed it
In lots of different ways.

You always had the answer
To life's great mystery.
You calmed me down when overwrought
And brought back peace to me.

How can I, a Granny now
Be half as wise as you?
Will I ever find the strength
To stay calm all life through?

Mum, I still feel like a child
When I think of your face.
The Mum I'll love with all my heart
Until my dying days.

Helen Strangwige

ELEGY TO HEARTBREAK

You always brought me flowers - roses, carnations.
Sometimes a sweet bouquet of wild flowers
Picked on an evening walk.
A sprig of apple blossom in the spring - and once,
When all the world seemed to be grey and dead,
A little piece of sacred mistletoe, found in a secret place.
You filled my days with light and fragrant warmth,
My nights with love that only soulmates know.
Your spirit left one golden summer's day,
I held your hand, but even all my love and all the strength
That I have ever had, could not prevail and keep you here with me.
I'd brought you flowers those weary pain-filled days.
And by the bed a vase of roses stood, and on the floor a single
                                        broken bloom;
Its fragile message like a dagger's thrust.
That was the moment that I felt my heart break, and saw the
                                        endless hours
Stretch out before me - a deserted road.
I dare not dream of you, my only love
For if I did I could not bear to wake
And find you were no longer there with me.

Shelagh Ansell

CHRISTOPHER

*(For My son Christopher,
born and fell asleep on the 19th May 1987)*

Never had too much time to know you at all,
For the Lord called your name, and you answered his call.
You were my little boy, you were my second son,
I sat cuddling you, together, we watched the rise of the sun.

You were two hours old, but you couldn't stay long,
The angels were singing your name in their song.
The doctors and nurses had all done their best,
But they couldn't delay your eternal rest!

I told you your name, your mum's and your brothers'
Spoke of myself, and one or two others.
Told you all of the things I felt you should know,
Before the awful time came, when I knew you must go.

Your tiny eyes opened, just once, for a glance,
At a world where you'd never at all have a chance
To laugh and to play, or to grow like your brother,
You were destined, my son, to belong to another.

You ascended to Heaven, and I cried bitter tears,
The memories stayed with me through all of the years.
How I held you so close, from your moment of birth,
'til the angels escorted you upwards from earth.

Sun shone on the hills as we laid you to rest,
I tried to be strong, at least, did my best.
I believed that a power much greater than me,
Wanted you near him, that's how it must be.

Asleep now my sweet baby, you reside with the Lord,
Alive in the sanctuary his love doth afford.
But you'll always be here too, asleep in my heart,
As you fell asleep then Son, in my arms, at the start.

Brian L Porter

IN MEMORY OF CAROLINE

She was sublime my dearest Caroline.
Will I ever see her again?
Before it was now,
Now it is then.
Tender loving and true
Her wishes, her thoughts I knew.
Together we got married my wife she became,
What I did was to change her name.
I became a father and she a mother too
And gradually up our family grew.
To me she was everything
Now her praises sing.
I must face the world again with grit
And I think of what she accomplished
                when I contemplate and sit.
She would not want me to mope
But carry on life with hope.
Sadly with us no more
I did her adore.
I must say that I am very glad
That all these years her I had.
What is written here is a poem
                for her in rhymes
To remember together that we had
                wonderful times.

Allan John Mapstone

FRANKIE

You wore your whiskers almost fluted
At the ends: an act of defiance undiluted,
Your missing teeth gave you
The semblance of a smile,
And yet even while you were sleeping
All the while you were scheming
How to ridicule your human pet.
Stealing from the fridge and table,
Chasing spiders up the curtains
Till they were certain to shiver and fall
In velvet folds at my feet.
Then on padded paws slowly pacing across the room
To occupy my most comfortable chair,
Sitting there as though
You had been seated serenely for hours
And knew nothing of mischief.
Sadly your appointed hour came
But left behind was more
Than your name,
Your darting eyes, toothless gums, whiskered face
And sheer audacity fondly remembered
Live on in your empty space.

Pat Isiorho

HAROLD BLENKINSOP MY FRIEND

Some sad news came my way today
That Harold Blenkinsop had passed away;
He was a man so good and kind,
No better friend could you find!

A railwayman with a heart of gold
Who helped the young and the old.
He really was one of the best;
I pray for him now he's at rest.

Sometimes we met in the street,
With a smile he would me greet;
'Hello Frank,' he then would say.
'It's nice to see you this good day.'

We would then talk of times past,
Of memories that will always last,
About the good times we both had.
It was great to work with this man!

I thank the Lord for my friend;
Memories of him will never end.
Here in my heart he'll forever stay.
Same sad news came my way today.

Francis Allen

FOR MARGARET

This is the time when we would wander through
The woods, and by the sea. Oh sea of dreams!
And land of light, of mystery; with gleams
Of splendour from beyond the cloudless blue.
The wide sky hides the place where now you dwell;
This sun but pale reflection of pure light.
These breezy hills, and the deep, tossed to white
Crests of great waves, this wind and ocean-swell
Tell of the glory of the unknown shore;
There, where bright beams of shimmering, finest gold
And rainbows, veil the hills, and evermore
High summer reigns as in the days of old
Do you still wander through the fields of flowers?
Do you see our wild spring from those green bowers?

Diana Momber

TO SHEILA

For all those years when we were heart to heart,
Soulmates; for all the little intimate moments
We shared in our own private world apart.
For every remembered smile, for each sweet thought,
For your gracefulness, for the way you were unaware
How your beauty of face and mind together, were caught
In a radiance that shone upon my ordinary life;
So I was twice the man that I otherwise might have been;
And so proud that the world should know you as my wife.
My Sheila, I loved you.

But no one can know just how broken my heart was made
To suffer with you in the recent tortured years;
To see your sweet personality gradually fade,
To see your desperate struggles to stay in control,
While depression dragged you ever more down and down,
Till you felt you had lost God's presence in a deep, black hole.
For those years when I could not ease your sorrow and pain,
Now ended because, Dear Heart, you could take no more,
I grieve; but I know that in Heaven we'll meet again.
For those years, *even more,* my Sheila, I love you.

John

DAD

I close my eyes, and I can see
You walking down the street.
And I would run, and you would catch
And twirl me off my feet.

I see you still, pipe in your mouth,
A twinkle in your eye.
Thin, wiry, always hard at work
No task too hard to try.

To me so kind and generous,
A rock in times of strife.
Without you I would not exist
For you Dad gave me life.

So thank you for the love you gave
So unconditionally.
And death has only placed you Dad,
One step in front of me.

Margaret Fisher

A TRICK OF LIGHT

Then my love came unexpectedly one night
Imagination maybe - a trick of light?
Waiting patiently, one knee bent head lifted -
Caught in a moonbeam - before the clouds drifted
And partially shaded the garden again
Shrouding the standing figure in misty rain.
A dream perhaps yet the pain was as a blast
I imagined faded, buried in the past,
Or was he waiting patiently as always,
(Resignedly accepting the lonely days)
And had I run and kissed his cold ghostly face
Enfolded me in a passionate embrace,
Yes, my love came unexpectedly one night
Or did he? Just an old dream - a trick of light.

Rosemary Langdon

EMOTIONS

Sweet small pleasures
Looks of love
The touch of hands
Our baby's first sweet smile
Our children's breathless laughter
Silence when no need for words
Your soft and gentle sigh
Tears of sadness when we're apart
Tears of joy when reunited
Peace.

A F Bell

NO LONGER NEED TO QUESTION

When the flame of passion
goes.
The fire becomes a
glow.
When the warmth of two
hands clasping means
more than one can
know.
When the years go swiftly
by, and the minds are not
so clear,
The comfort is contentment
knowing you are
near.
When in love, is never
questioned
The knowledge is so
clear,
A flame gives so much
heat, but so much
comfort gives a
glow.

M Rossi

THE LOVE GAME BALLAD

The wonder of the music
born as ballads in
their time,
Composers wrote of
lovers and of sweethearts
all in rhyme,
Of the garden and
the little seat where
all things come
to mind and love is
not regarded as
any kind of crime.
I do not see why we
should fear that
crying is a shame
for ladies try it all
the time it becomes
their little game.

V N King

FOR JIMMY

It was always so special, why couldn't it be?
The love that I had for you; you had for me.
We thought that for ever those good times would last,
What happened that now they are all in the past?
We walked hand in hand in the sun's golden light,
In cool mystic shadows we whispered goodnight.
When frost-sparkled air set the roof tops aglow
We watched brilliant stars watching us here below.
We laughed in the showers; we first met in the rain.
I even now dream it could happen again.
And bombs fell, and friends died and homes blew away,
And only our love stayed the same day by day.
How could I have known on a cold Christmas Eve,
That you, my dear soldier, were on your last leave?
All so long ago now, so much come and gone
So why does the memory go on, on and on -
And how can the love that was once you and I
Become lost forever and yet never die?

D Rhodes

TREASURED MEMORIES IN A BROKEN HEART

Times we shared
Times I've cared
Time leaves you unprepared
Time left me, Alone and scared

Time so much time
Time is all I have
Time to reminisce
Time for sadness or a laugh

Time for me to recall
Time to cry, done it all
Time to die, no time to fall
Time to escape from it all

Time for love
Time for joy
Time to rise above
Time for me and my boy

Time to breathe
Time to leave
Time to change
The way I perceive

Time; Precious not always kind
Time to clear these cobwebs from my mind . . .

Donna Hardie

THE TAXI

We sat in the taxi tonight
Side by side,
Not touching,
Feeling.

Polite chat with the driver.
Sitting close,
Not touching,
Feeling.

We stopped close to your house
(not too close).
Warm, kind lips,
You kissed me
With feeling.

Joan M Smith

LOVE IS . . .

Love is the feeling of tingling bliss
That floods through the veins at the first long kiss.

Love is the trust that two people share
through good times and bad times that shows they care

Love is the gift of a brand new life,
when two kindred souls become man and wife

Love is the happiness families bring
Love is the strength that binds everything.

Eileen Martin

ALWAYS TOGETHER

I had a love which would last forever
a love that blossomed when we were together
A love we thought, that for the rest of our life
would overcome all troubles, sorrow and strife
But our future was not meant to be
you were sent away for King and country
and like so many others, you never returned
and my memories of you have forever burned,
in my soul, in my life and in my heart
for the time has come now never to be apart.

Carole Hoy

The Madness

Always keep the passion,
for there must always be passion.
Even in the end
when the world falls apart
and every dream like the body
Is bruised and hurting.
For if I could live this life again
I would still fall into her,
into unrequited love.
Where the briefest of moments
are worth a thousand years alone.

Michael Wilson

THE LOVE OF WHAT YOU ARE AND WHY: EVERYTHING YOU WISH I'LL BE FOR YOU

Just to be back with sweet Jeannie
Precious gift please hear my plea
Won't you say you still care for me
You know I just want to make you happy.

Jeannie Jeannie don't make me blue
For you know I love you true
Oh how I need to be back with you
As it was before with love ever new.

Now wherever you are or may be
I'm like a lone sailor on stormy sea
Thinking of you as time goes by
In the love of what you are and why.

The second time around with you
Can still be the best it's true
If only we can relight the flame
Burning again bright in love's own aim.

The fairest woman I've ever known
With never ever a sad moan or groan
Leading me to your golden throne
In sweet love's pleasure zone.

There is the loveliness of you
When all sweet joy came into view
Fair is the wonder in all I see
Knowing that you still care for me.

Oh to move closer to you every day
Jeannie Jeannie doing things your way
Everything you wish I'll be for you
Jeannie Jeannie don't make me blue
For you know I love you true
Oh how I need to be back with you . . .

Johnnie Docherty

UNTITLED

What would you say
If I said I'm happy?
You are all I've ever needed
But has our psyche
Over-ridden our love
And what matters been superseded?
I fall in love more
When I see you smile
You've provoked reactions of grandeur
I've found my goal
I've found my girl
And I'm so happy that I've found you.

Sid Stovold

WHERE THE HEART LIES

Standing on the top of the hill,
seeing the beauty of the glen,
feeling the breath of morning chill,
hearing a grouse calling his hen.

The fir clad sides, gently sloping
down to softly waving heather,
watching the burn, quietly hoping
we shall meet and be together.

Hearing a sound that fills the air,
the haunting pipes lifting my heart,
catching sight of my man so fair,
knowing now we shall never part.

With feet barely touching the ground,
joyfully I rush to his side,
held in his arms, feel his heart pound,
come tomorrow, I'll be his bride.

A Odger

MY CONFESSION

From being just a little, only child,
'Twas evident that females drive me wild!
Now, since these feelings cannot be reviled,
I find them in my outsize heart all piled.

I love to keep them safe within my clutch,
And openly confess - since this be such -
Perchance, I really love them all too much;
Those sweet, kind words and gentle, velvet touch.

As one through crazy adolescence steers,
With all these different girls, through all those years,
The countless lovely smiles - yet so few tears -
I've always loved to treat my darling dears.

Love's golden rose still buds, although time flies;
The longest, fairest hair and grey-blue eyes.
This hoard of treasured love in my heart lies;
Such wondrous beauty shall I ever prize!

To those who kindly feel inclined to stress
That, in their view, my love-life seems a mess,
Methinks - they envy me my happiness!
And after all, at least I did confess!

Gareth Wynne Richards

EVEN IF WE ARGUE...

I really don't think you've ever heard me say,
How much I appreciate you, and miss you when you're away,
You're there when I need you and life seems grey,
You cheer me up on the unhappiest day,
Even when I'm nasty, you put up with me!
And I hope soon you'll begin to see,
How much I love you,
And I always will.

Harriet Forkin

RELIGHT THE FIRE OF YESTERDAY:
DON'T LEAVE LOVE LEFT UNSAID

It was just a plastic bag with memories now all denied
Which left me shattered with such sad tears inside
You left it on my doorstep on an early March morn
Leaving me left outside crying all lost and forlorn.

A couple of musical souvenirs hardly ever played:
One or two pictures no longer on your wall displayed
I gave them to you when we were so sweetly in love
Which now for some sad reason you've given the shove.

Oh to be back on an early September summer day
Before the fateful beauty of autumn leaves held sway
Looking into your misty eyes of deep azure blue
Holding hands together again as we so often used to do.

Now as spring of a new year beckons with daffodils in bloom
You've left me all alone again with cloudy skies of gloom
I guess I took you for granted as I once did long ago
And to lose you yet again I just don't want to know.

You told me that it's all over and you've found someone new!
But is this really the truth my love or just another cue?
For you know I'll always love you no matter what you say
So please give me another chance sweet angel and never fly away.

Is it so wrong to try to relight the fire of yesterday?
When we never cared about tomorrow whatever came our way
I know one shouldn't always let the heart control the head
But sometimes it's better to be that way than leave love left unsaid.

I know it's been a long winter and spring is late to come
But before you know it darling we'll be sparkling in the sun
So don't give up now on what we both want and need to do
And tell your new lover it's time to say adieu!

Our own new love is just beginning and spring is in the air
So say goodbye to winter's frost and hello to a springtime
love affair . . .

Jackie Docherty

HANDS OF TIME

Seventeen years now we still meet
Our fleeting conversations on the street

Our situations never seem to change
We both smile all the same

I've often wondered is she aware
Just how much - I still care.

As if a silent language
We still seem to share

My teenage dream girl
She still makes my head twirl

Instantly I begin to reminisce
Our one embrace and passionate kiss

The lingering look upon her face
All those years still longing to embrace.

This empty space - her angelic face

Time tracks on both growing older

Should I throw caution to the wind
Tell her of my true feelings within

Test the strength of time
Ask for her hand in mine?

Graham Hare

Cousin Ron - His Parents' Battle Of Grief

Ron was his name, a clever boy,
He was his parents' pride and joy.
He was only just a man
When the second world war began.
The Royal Air Force he decided to try,
Before very long he began to fly.
Across the channel the planes would go,
Bombs to drop, to defeat the foe.
Day by day his parents' hearts would stop,
When the bombs began to drop.

This young man was so brave and strong,
But he was to die before too long.
Shot down in a foreign land
His parents could not be on hand.
Their grief they carried many a year,
This was always their worst fear.

His father died in middle age,
Still unable to see his grave.
His mother lived with a broken heart,
All her dreams were torn apart,
In later years when the war was won,
To have the love and comfort of her only son.
His name was Ronald Dobbins, and if you see,
Grave 9, plot 11, row K in Durnbach war cemetery.
Please say a prayer for them and me.

Barbara Stanczyszyn

LOST LOVE

My old companion
      whose name I know so well
appears again before my eyes
      in the midnight darkness.

Cloaked and full of foreboding
      he stirs the dying embers
of the love that lost its way.

He shows me my unhappy heart
      which desperately tries
to hold together
      the shattered fragments
of a lovely dream.

He points to my sad and lonely soul
      to the wrenching pain
and the howling grief.

He stands with me, as hollow eyed
      bereft and forlorn I gaze
at your receding form.

I cried . . . don't go . . . don't go.
      My hands stretched out
to hold you back,
      but all I had left to hold
were the ashes and embers
      of the love that lost its way.

The name of my cloaked friend?
      he is known as dark despair.
His shadowed form surrounds me
      to hide the love that lost its way.

Brigitta D'Arcy

PENDING

I filed you away yesterday,
Memories stored and put away,
No more your letters on my desk,
I'll clear my mind, time to rest,
Bittersweet into the file,
Out of my head to stay awhile,
Tidy desk, no more to glance,
No more to tempt, to take a chance,
Maybe your letters should be shred,
Pending - In the file instead.

W Curran

THE DAWNING

What is it about death that we all fear,
Is it the pain and suffering when near,
Is it the loss of the love of our life,
All that was gained in our struggle through life.

I've seen you at work, I don't like your style,
Your hideous job I truly revile,
You cast your net wide forever to hold,
Taking the lives of the young and the old.

I've know your pain and the despair,
You've taken my dad, how he died wasn't fair,
His body once strong became twisted and painful,
His mind once clear became sad and neglectful.

I've since seen him clear in a dream one night,
His lovely face gave me delight,
No words were spoken, no touch was made,
But on his face content was laid and I knew then our peace was made.

Now I've seen through your darkness, my sadness gone,
Before me a brightness, a light, the true one,
The glow which is constant, a message of care,
A wondrous story which I want to share.

God is with us, so do not despair.

So when life is ending and our time is near,
Let me reassure you there's nothing to fear,
Move forward in freedom with peace and content,
For this is a story which always was meant.

While writing these lines a new light is dawning,
I've been working too long where last breaths are drawing,
It's time to collect, to consider my yearning,
Maybe it's the humanist in me which is stirring.

Olivia Harris

BEST FRIEND

(For George who slipped away
While no one was looking . . .)

An exquisite feeling smacked me
I forget about everything hum-drum.
Fixes me, mends me, loves me.
Better than any mortal.
Never lets me down.
Never intimidates.
Only ingratiates itself to me.
Fills me with extensive peace.
No hassle, no problem, no nothing.
It has stolen many things from me.
Once was pretty and free.
Had children, a man who loved me.
Had a house, a home, a car.
Nice gold things, nice clothes, nice skin.
I am taken body and soul,
I have sold both for my love, my life.
Standing alone, just me and it, it and me.
Lying, crying, dying.
Here are my works, my imminent relief.
An exquisite feeling smacked me . . .

D P R

A LITTLE MEDITATION ON LIFE AND LOVE

Sometimes we find it hard to say the things that
really matter in life. The things we should truly
say to our husband, daughter, son or wife.
But we fail, we fall short of the mark.

We hurt each other with unkind words that we
never really meant to say. So stop and think for
a moment, we never speak to our friends this way,
only to the ones we love.

Does true love have to be such a hurtful thing
that tears and love go hand in glove.
A little more effort could mean a few less tears to dry.
For the sake of peace and harmony please just try.

Think on this, if you've got nothing nice to say
don't say anything at all. Try hard to maintain
the peace and pray for those who fall.

Robert Waggitt

BEWILDERMENT

Indeterminate changes over a period of time
Observed by me, are so hard to define
In a husband whose always been happy, carefree
And now his confusion is frightening me.
One day happy, another day sad . . .
Oh! dear, what is happening
Am I going mad?
The droop of his shoulders . . . the lost look in his eye
And for some hidden reason, he can't tell me why.
Wandering off, he cannot explain
The lapses he has to add to his pain.
Repeating his questions he cannot remember
Is it July, or is it December?

Bemused, bewildered, we seek a prognosis,
The hospital may, provide a diagnosis.

'Alzheimer's disease, are you quite sure?'
I really don't think I can take anymore
But saddened, we struggle through the long slow decline,
The husband that once was
Is no longer mine.

D Lloyd

IT'S OVER

Of love what do I know
The years of closeness, life together of years that pass and grow.
The smile, the touch, the eyes that shine to one another's spoken line.
Soulmates joined as if forever would speak of parting - never, never.
What changes from that safe illusion and brought us to this

sad conclusion

Not touching and cold are the hands that were warm.
Eyes now not seeing and words full of scorn.
When did this happen
When did this change
Two people so close and now so strange
What can a heart do to ease the pain
What can one do to start again
Too many years are gone and lost
And now the years to count the cost
Oh love so wonderful, but was only to borrow
I never thought forever would end tomorrow.

Sonia Sacre

A LAST VISIT

Her eyes traced my memories
Like an old lullaby
Into a jeweller's box
Without the place names of youth.

Her season blushed,

I'd wait for no other summer:
She'd opened a flower
With the power of cancer
Bathed in my oxygen.

Marylène Walker

WHEN MOONS MUCH

The sun rises, blissful.
But for a soul, simple;
Another, in slow deaths.

The sun rises,
Soul hugs,
And sails up, noon;
Then descent,
To farewells, so much harry.

This, in chain,
Of days, claustrophobically unchanging;
Hunting for meaning,
When season, numb.

First there was dream,
Then, investment.
The hope,
Ah! The prayer;
Emancipating post.

But where lies console,
When moons much;
Same old dreary roll.

Hope wilts,
And descent finds;
Sail into lapse.
Spirit, a delicate teardrop.

Prayer, mature transformation.
No longer plea, for specific time-tabled desire.

In humility; to the All Knowing,
Give of self, to Wisdom's Eternal.

On a simple day,
Sunrise, channelling in, love vibrant.

Rowland Warambwa

DRIFTING OUT OF SIGHT

All we know is the passing of the time,
And we see, shadows on the doorstep.
No one really knows, how you spend your day,
But drifting out of sight, never was the way.

In and out, the phasing of your life,
Finding out the reasons don't come easy,
Only time can tell and no one else can say,
But drifting out of sight never was the way.

Read your mind which no one else can do,
Think it out, the magic's in the moment,
Leave it all too late and everyone will say,
That drifting out of sight never was the way.

Don't know what it is that makes you smile,
Can you take your mind back for a while,
Maybe it is worth another mile.

John Cook

WHO CARES FOR THE CARER

The day's gone so fast.
From the first client to the last.
Listened to all of their plights
(And told of the family fights!)

When you've washed your last face
Put everything back in its place
Closed the last door
(And your feet feel so sore!).

You arrive at your gate
Yes, you are a half an hour late!
Sit down in your chair for a rest
Knowing you've done your very best.

A cup of tea and a kiss
That won't go amiss.
Gives a big hug and a smile
Makes caring worthwhile.

Muriel Turner

THE FIVE MONTH UNBORN CHILD

The specialist said, 'It's quite alright',
giving his mass-market smile on that
(I wanted to believe him) crowded afternoon;
foolish man, what did he know of the common life . . .
crowded, cramped, overheated trains,
walking on hot macadam in blazing heat
with a child pining to be plucked and cradled,
we sit on the sand, watch husband and daughter
in the cool water, on the hot afternoon, unable to enter,
can I ever forgive you, you and you
innocent of all but ignorance;
forgive the dragging down-ness
after the hot afternoon, forgive the loss and the death,
the foetid ward and medics with
dated mistrusted deeds of mistrust;
who can I forgive, for no one,
for no one, protected me or him;
I only know my son is gone
unburied, no rites or rights of mourning -
never forgotten, always the pain
in the hot afternoon,
the grief cries to be acknowledged,
and yet, twenty years on
what else can there be but forgiveness,
and suddenly the pain is gone . . .

Monica Redhead

MY FRIEND

She fights her daily battles
Her daily grind is long
But she has an inner peace of mind
For her faith in God is strong.

She always wears a happy smile
This dear friend of mine
Though life brings her many hardships
She says everything is fine.

I never hear her grumble
For her policy you see
Is - There is always someone somewhere
Who is much worse off than me.

Even though she's often racked with pain
And she cannot leave her chair
She takes comfort from her friendly lift
Her helpmate on the stair.

Though her hands are bent twisted
With no strength in hip and thigh
She is nature's secret tonic
With a twinkle in her eye.

Her courage strong puts me to shame
For I never see her sad
Her presence so inspires me
When my own day has been bad.

Oh how I love this precious friend
Dear soul of loving care
I wouldn't swap her for the world
And for me she's always there.

Barbara Davies

TO THINK OF YOU

The sun setting in the sky
Leaves falling from a tree
When loved ones are taken from us
Their faces we cannot see

The first raindrop from the clouds
The fall of winter snow
A person to remember
Afraid to let feelings show

A candle running out of light
A flower wilting in the sun
Scared to miss everybody
Frightened to have some fun

A new born baby smiling
An early morning dew
Are things we should remember
To always think of you.

Angela Plater

EASTBOURNE DISTRICT GENERAL HOSPITAL
PATTERNS OF PROFESSIONALISM

Flowers of colourful, artistic display,
Charming the entrance, welcoming pleasure,
Reception attention, concern at hand,
Genuine interest, a helpful measure.

Atmosphere of instant warmth,
Essence, hot coffee, nourishing health.
Dealing with people, sharing and caring,
Displaying comforts, a mindful wealth.

Patients await, with time to observe,
Conversation develops, reflections emerge,
Comparing ailments, a source of reserve.
Realising averages, a hopeful surge.

Apprehension may surface, quell its request,
Confirmed guidance, trained to know best.
Kindness conveyed, revealed peace of mind,
Patients response, smiling spirited find.

Nurses the anchorage, smartly primed,
Presenting an image, confidently timed,
Aiming to help, everyone's request,
Reassurance given, a kindling blessed . . .

Lorna Tippett

LOVE

Love is a friend,
That beats in your heart,
Love is a fiend,
That rips you apart,
Love is a feeling,
That makes you feel whole,
Love is a force,
That tears at your soul,
Love is a tonic,
That fills you with life,
Love is a blade,
That cuts like a knife,
Love is a passion,
That makes us all shout,
Love is a pleasure,
We can't live without.

D Woodford

THE GIFT

'Tis pleasant to receive flowers
Which ease life's pressures
And replenishes the mind
Folk feeling sublime

Their blooms of creative art
Go straight to the heart
Giving pleasure to folk alone
Especially is known

The flowers so colourful
Are pleasing to all
And when artistically arranged
What more can be said!

Gardens in every county
Are fascinating to see
Each it's own style
And a different angle

'Tis magnificent to see
As one will agree
A carefully arranged design
'Enhances' the mind

To someone in sorrow
As one will know
A 'Gift' of scented flowers
Fills them with pleasure

As everyone will agree
'Flowers' are a joy to see
With their beautiful colours and scents
And are seen in all 'events'.

Josephine Foreman

ARE YOU HERE DADDY?

Are you here Daddy . . .

> when my head is throbbing so much that it hurts to think?

> when my eyes ache so much that they feel like they are going to pop out of my head?

> when I simply cannot cry anymore because I have no tears left?

> when my sobs have subsided and I lie here exhausted?

> when I need someone to trust, who will listen and comfort?

Please . . .

> fold Your arms of love around me,

> cradle me against Your breast,

> rock me to sleep and in doing so . . .

> refresh me to face the storm with You holding my hand!

Margi Hughes

JUST ASK

We mourn the dead
With monuments
With flowers of earthy love,
We drown in grief
Our peace of Mind
Which rests in Heaven Above.
The earth is but
A school of thought -
We're here for just a time
And only the power of God
Can save -
Didn't Jesus calm the storm?
Yet still today
His presence near
If we but understand -
The storms through life
He'd help to sway,
Bring peaceful interlude.
And so He calms
Each trusting heart
If we but ask in prayer,
Continuous throughout
years on Earth -
Forever - he is near.

Mary Skelton

I WISH

I wish I could hold you in my arms,
or sit you on my knee,
I wish you could call to see me
and stay for a home-made tea.
I wish I could read you a story,
or tuck you up in bed,
but none of these wishes will come true
because heaven called for you instead.
So dance with the stars my darling,
sing with the moonbeams too,
sit beside Jesus he will take care of you.
But when I come and join you my wishes will all
come true, as together we will
dance with the stars my darling,
we will sing with the moonbeams too,
together we will sit beside sweet Jesus
then Nana will take care of you.

Carol Gallipoli

THOSE WHO LOST NOW FOUND

I have felt the hand of the devil within my soul at bay
likened to the speed of a rain fed ford, with the roar of the Milky Way.
Penetrating this mist of anger one calms to the mysterious sound
of voices, calling from the outer world, imperious and profound.
These words of the Lord come settle gently upon the mind
as does a feather floating serenely on the stream to live and lie reclined.
To make one think clearly with no distracting influence.
Grand in its simplicity and deeper in its significance
the fears and worries burst forth to go as if some warrior laid to rest.
With the spirits of the stars one goes onward with renewed zest
hand in hand with angels to girdle faith's new sound,
God's hand of love stretching out to those who lost, now found.

John Clarke

IT's Me Against The World

When I need God, he needs me.
We search for each other, equally.
But I'm the only one that's found,
I shrink myself down to the ground,
In hope that soon I will dissolve,
And all my life shall be resolved.
One blink is all it takes I find,
To see my human from behind,
And when I do, my eyes awake,
Back to the land of my mistakes.
So stress builds up behind my eyes,
And once again my body dies.
I'll never break the web I'm in,
It's there to keep me suffering.
Share happy moments, yes I may,
They can't last longer than a day,
So on the floor I shall stay curled,
Because it's me against the world.

Alexa Konik

TO LIVE WITH PARKINSON'S

To live with Parkinson's is a constant struggle,
My life sometimes gets in a muddle.
I try my best to kick back and fight,
But sometimes it's hard when your steam runs out.
This illness is very hard to explain,
The constant quality is hard to retain.
One minute you feel you could run a mile,
Sometimes it's a struggle to even raise a smile.
I try very hard to push myself,
I'd give away my money if I had my health.
My mind goes blank, eyes poor of sight,
I can't turn over in bed at night.
I lose the ability to concentrate,
And help you will soon appreciate.
I fight and struggle, it's an upward hill,
But never mind I've got my pill.
They talk about a Dopamine in a patch,
The effect like a pill I hope will match.
It would be nice not to worry anymore,
Do I take my pill, or did I take it before?
There's lots of help from the Parkinson's Society
And you'll make new friends, with this caring charity
I know there's no cure at the present time,
But the research is good, and right on line.
To the Medical Conferences I like to go,
Because one day soon they'll tell me there's a cure.
The outlook is good, and there's lots of scope,
God willing I'll battle on, and live in hope.

Keep smiling.

Linda Garner

FADING LIGHT

The daylight is fading from my eyes
Days are long and so are the nights
I am going blind and cannot see
What is going wrong with me?
I will soon be in despair
If I cannot see round everywhere
Will folks ease my mind
Or shut me out and be unkind
I will learn to get around
Not stuck in here and be house-bound
If I can't watch TV
I'll listen to my tapes and CD
In my mind I will go away
To lands very far away.

In the dark but wide awake
There are many others like me
Who are blind and cannot see
How do others cope
With friends help I hope
I don't like this world of dark
No more walks in the park
I need someone to be my guide
To hold my arm by my side
Another day I'll use my stick.

One day I will buy a dog to guide
Walking here by my side
Who will be a friend to me
Now my eyes do not see
I still like the birds at dawn
Feeling the sun when it is warm
I have to make the best of things
Whatever each new day does bring.

Sheila Waller

MY ROSE

Through my sad loss my grief is great,
I miss my Rose, my wife, my mate
No more to kiss her tender face
Hear her sweet voice, no more embrace
Our love was all we had to give
With her on earth, so much to live
Her gentle smile, so full of fun,
Enjoyed at work, by everyone
Her thoughts of others, in tender care
The friendliness she loved to share
A tender mother who loved her son,
Her just reward, so proud of one
To feel her near and guide me true
Until my days in life are through
And we are joined our hand in hand
In Heaven's Kingdom and Eternal Land
Through my sad loss my grief is great
I miss my Rose, my wife, my mate.

E L Hannam

UNTITLED

Although, my sweet, it is some years, in truth,
Since that fateful day, saw you depart!
So leaving me to grieve, with broken heart,
For all the days and nights since then
I have wandered in my mind, so lost in life,
Knowing that we'll never meet again,
But always appearing in my dreams,
You come and kiss my lips as if alive.

In my bed I lay, sleepless, gazing at the stars
To wonder which one is shining there,
And if it could be you, sweetheart,
That hung it out to light my way to you!
In my mind, you are the same as then,
You'll never change, but I am failing,
Growing old, losing the way that I was then,
When we were together and in love.

R G Hammond

TO MY NAN

You advised, you consoled, you made no fuss
Any problem with you I could discuss
To cope with life with your guiding hand
I grew from boyhood into a man
You were my mentor and my guide
Oh, how it upset me the day you died
When times were hard and money low
You always found threepence to ease the blow
When you won some money, you and Pa
Treated me to my first and only guitar
And when need for school clothes came around
Wool for a new jumper was always found
Knitted into a garment overnight
New jumper next morning blue and bright
Small jolly smiling lady with soft silver hair
For thirty years of my life you were there
I was unable to be there when you had your fall
So I could not say 'Goodbye' when that was all
                              that was left
Nan, I miss your loving care
But you never left me, in my heart you're always here.

Mike Jackson

ABERFAN

How gently now life's river flows
Though evenings scented air
I was searching for a part of me
That took some comfort there

A place where once time stood still
Cast silhouettes of sweet repose
And conscience woke with heavy heart
Like a teardrop from a wilting rose.

I saw in the fading light of day
The love they'd lost love they'd found
The wasted years that slipped away
Entombed within this hallow ground

For I was but myself a child
When birds of darkness flew unseen
To find the words to reason why
And stand upon this valley green

No longer do the pit wheels turn
To echo through these empty vales
How can I understand the pain
Of Aberfan - children of Wales.

R M Robson

SUBMISSIONS INVITED
SOMETHING FOR EVERYONE

POETRY NOW 2001 - Any subject,
any style, any time.

WOMENSWORDS 2001 - Strictly women,
have your say the female way!

STRONGWORDS 2001 - Warning!
Age restriction, must be between 16-24,
opinionated and have strong views.
(Not for the faint-hearted)

All poems no longer than 30 lines.
Always welcome! No fee!
Cash Prizes to be won!

Mark your envelope (eg *Poetry Now*) *2001*
Send to:
Forward Press Ltd
Remus House, Coltsfoot Drive,
Peterborough, PE2 9JX

OVER £10,000 POETRY PRIZES
TO BE WON!

Judging will take place in October 2001